ROSEMARY-MARGARI

ANIMAL REMAINS
IN ARCHAEOLOGY

Cover photograph

Cat skull.
(Photograph: G. Owen,
Department of Archaeology, Cambridge University.)

Published by
SHIRE PUBLICATIONS LTD
Cromwell House, Church Street, Princes Risborough,
Aylesbury, Bucks HP17 9AJ, UK.

Series Editor: James Dyer

ISBN 0 85263 633 4

First published 1984

Set in 11 point Times and printed in Great Britain by
C. I. Thomas & Sons (Haverfordwest) Ltd,
Press Buildings, Merlins Bridge, Haverfordwest, Dyfed.

Contents

Preface

This book provides an introduction to the subject of animal remains in archaeology for the interested student and layman and summarises some of the main problems encountered when analysing faunal material, for the benefit of the archaeologist. The text contains many technical terms which may be unfamiliar to readers and they are advised to consult frequently the Glossary (chapter 11).

I am extremely grateful to my husband, Dr T. Hooley, who has been a source of encouragement and has made many useful comments concerning this work. I would like to thank Professor P. Jewell and Dr P. Mellars, of Cambridge University, for kindly providing photographs. Most of the photography was undertaken by Mr G. Owen, Department of Archaeology, Cambridge University, and I am most appreciative of his work. I thank the Trustees of the British Museum for permission to reproduce photographs, the Faculty of Archaeology and Anthropology and the Museum of Zoology, Cambridge University. Finally I am indebted to Knuth who provided the inspiration for this work.

List of illustrations

1
Introduction

The animal remains studied in archaeology include insects, parasites, molluscs, mites, mummies, coprolites, bird shells, wool, hair and hide remnants, together with the bones of mammals, reptiles, amphibians, birds and fish. In analysing these biological residues, the zooarchaeologist aims to reveal information about the life and habitat of prehistoric and historic man. Topics covered can embrace diet, hunting and butchery practices, religious rites, animal husbandry, season of site occupation, local environment, dating techniques, climate and technologies, e.g. bone, antler, hide and glue.

A large section of the book is devoted to mammal bone since this is the most common zoological material recovered from archaeological excavations. It is important to realise that many animal bones collected from excavations are the by-products of experimental diggings conducted for other reasons. Probably all the data for Romano-British and later towns has been unearthed on this basis.

Further, there can be staggering variations in sample size between different chronological periods; for instance British Roman and medieval town sites have produced enormous quantities of bone while British palaeolithic sites have nothing of comparable size. The main reason for this is that many of the stone age deposits, particularly from the Lower Palaeolithic, are derived deposits, that is the artefacts have been removed from their original place of resting and washed into sediments by a combination of fluviatile, lacustrine and aeolian activity.

However, problems can arise with having too large a sample. It has been estimated that to analyse all the bone from the Franchthi Cave in Greece would take one worker forty to fifty years. This mesolithic/neolithic site was carefully sieved in order to extract as many minute fragments of bone as possible. The cost effectiveness of analysing sites as large as this must be carefully examined by comparing the possible worth of the results with the huge amount of human effort needed.

The zoological remains should not be studied in isolation but in conjunction with the available documentary and iconographic evidence. In this book many examples of animal remains will be given from different prehistoric and historic periods. Fig. 1 provides a chronological table.

Animal Remains in Archaeology

			AD 410
ROMAN			
			AD 43
IRON AGE			
			BC 750
BRONZE AGE			
			BC 2500
NEOLITHIC			
			BC 4500
MESOLITHIC	Flandrian	**i**	*Star Carr bc 7607* *bc 7538*
			bc 8300
UPPER PALAEOLITHIC	Devensian	**g**	*Torenewton*
			30,000 bp
MIDDLE PALAEOLITHIC	Ipswichian	**i**	
			100,000 bp
	Wolstonian	**g**	
LOWER PALAEOLITHIC	Hoxnian	**i**	*Swanscombe*
	Anglian	**g**	
	Cromerian		750.000 bp

Fig. 1. A brief chronology of British prehistory. Dates after 8300 bc are based on historical and/or radiocarbon measurements, recalibrated via dendrochronology. Dates before 8300 bc are based on radiocarbon measurements up to 30,000 bp, and before that calculation is attempted using geological evidence via the sequence of glacial/interglacial periods. These latter dates are highly speculative at present. **g** represents a glacial period; **i** represents an interglacial period.

2
Mammal bone

Dating

Animal bones and antlers are extremely valuable for dating archaeological sites, and by association other artefacts, particularly in the palaeolithic period, where very often datable material such as charcoal is absent. The best known technique is that of radiocarbon dating; this is a long and expensive process and therefore cannot be used on a great number of specimens. In essence the method works as follows: cosmic rays bombard nitrogen in the atmosphere producing carbon-14, a radioactive isotope of carbon. This is then assimilated by plants and subsequently animals into their biological structures. When the plant or animal dies, exchange of carbon in the form of carbon dioxide with the atmosphere stops and the carbon-14 decays to a much more stable isotope, carbon-12. The radioactivity of the carbon-14 can be measured and the relative proportions of carbon-14 and carbon-12 in the sample determined. Thus from the known rate of decay and the assumed initial proportions of carbon-14 and carbon-12 in the living biological specimen, the age of the sample can be calculated.

The major assumption of this method was that the carbon-14 reservoir in the atmosphere had not changed with time. This is now known to be untrue. However, radiocarbon dates of up to 6,500 years bp (before present, see Glossary) can be recalibrated using data derived from an independent source, wood which has been dated by dendrochronology. This is achieved by matching the proportion of carbon-14 in a sample with the proportion in tree-rings of known date.

At the Tenth International Radiocarbon Conference (August 1979, Berne and Heidelberg) it was proposed that a mass spectrometer should be used to count directly the carbon-14 atoms, instead of their radioactivity. Thus a smaller sample of material could be utilised, 1 to 100 milligrams as compared with the original 200 to 500 grams (7-18 ounces), and it was predicted that ages of up to 100,000 years bp could be reached. Bone tissue comprises about 75 per cent inorganic and 25 per cent organic material. The protein collagen makes up the greater part of the organic fraction and the inorganic fraction is composed of the bone mineral apatite. In contrast with apatite, collagen does not exchange carbon with the environment (i.e. buried bone) and is thus a more suitable dating material if properly purified.

In general the radiocarbon method can date material to a maximum limit of 70,000 years bp although 40,000 years is the figure more commonly reached. This is because the radioactivity of very old material becomes increasingly difficult to detect. Because of a scarcity of volcanic rocks in Britain, dating methods which could extend this range further back in time cannot be used, e.g. potassium-argon dating. However, an important method using the amino-acids in bone, amino-acid racemisation (see below), looks promising. The advantages of this technique are that only a few grams of bone are needed and the dating range extends from a few thousand years to several hundred thousand years bp.

The molecular structures of amino-acids of biological origin all have a certain symmetry and after death a spontaneous reorientation starts to produce an opposite symmetry. This racemisation (reduction to equal quantities of each symmetry) is completed in about a million years. Two variables affect the rate of reaction: temperature and leaching. The temperature variable can be eliminated by measuring the extent of racemisation in radiocarbon dated bones for a particular site. Leaching has proved an almost insurmountable problem but work carried out by Dr Kenneth King of Columbia University indicates that gamma-carboxyglutamic acid concentration is a potentially useful index of *in situ* leaching in fossil bones. There is an inverse correlation between the concentration of this substance and leaching intensity in modern bone under laboratory conditions.

Uranium/thorium dates of bone can potentially give figures in the range of 100,000 to 300,000 years bp but this method is still at its developmental stage.

One of the greatest unsolved archaeological problems is that of residual material, the mixing of artefacts from different periods. It is easy to imagine how this could have happened. For example, on a town site where people from later periods have dug ditches and pits into earlier features, Roman material can be found in later levels and modern matter can be found in Roman levels. However, it is difficult to determine whether this has happened, particularly with bone.

In this capacity relative dating, as devised by the late Dr Kenneth Oakley, is of great importance, particularly when dealing with early remains. Bone is analysed for fluorine, nitrogen and uranium content. The principal of the technique is that the fluorine and uranium contents of the mineral component of buried bone and teeth increase with age, whereas the organic component nitrogen decreases. Therefore comparisons of the fluorine, nitrogen and uranium contents of a buried bone or tooth of questionable age with the ranges of these elements present in other bones or teeth of known age and in similar matrix at the same site may indicate clearly the relative antiquity of the specimen.

This technique was applied with considerable success to remains from the Barnfield gravel pit, Swanscombe, Kent. In 1935 and 1936 Mr A. T. Marston discovered two human skull fragments 24 feet (7.3 m) below the surface in the Barnfield gravel pit. They lay near the base of the Upper Middle Gravels of the 100 foot (30 m) terrace of the river Thames. Many years later, in 1955, a third cranial fragment was found which matched the others. The skull bones were embedded in a sandy gravel which contained a mammalian fauna including the straight-tusked elephant *(Palaeoloxodon antiquus)*. On analysis, similar contents of nitrogen, fluorine and uranium were found in both the human and mammal bones, thus signifying that they were approximately contemporary. These are the oldest human bones found in Britain and could be about 250,000 years old although this date needs corroboration (see below).

Environment

Exotic animal remains have been uncovered from a number of British sites, for example a complete and articulated mammoth skeleton at Norwood Lane, Southall, London, which was associated with a Levalloisian flake-blade (weapon); hippopotamus and hyena at Trafalgar Square, London; hippopotamus at Barrington, Cambridgeshire (plate 1); mammoth at Ipswich; a hyena den at Wookey Hole in the Mendips; woolly rhinoceros, cave bear, mammoth and hyena at King Arthur's Cave, Herefordshire; reindeer, woolly rhinoceros and mammoth at Long Hole Cave, Glamorgan; mammoth at Wouldham, Kent (plate 2); and a whole skeleton of an elk at High Furlong, Lancashire, which was found with proto-Maglemosian barbed points (weapons). The hippopotamus occurred in Britain quite commonly during the palaeolithic period and has been found as far north as Stockton-on-Tees in Cleveland.

The palaeolithic period is characterised by several glacial phases when ice sheets covered much of Britain's surface, the most southerly extent being the Thames valley. The Anglian, Wolstonian and Devensian glacial phases correspond with the

Plate 1. Hippopotamus lower jawbone from Barrington, Cambridgeshire. Canine outer curvature length is 410 millimetres (16 inches).

Mindel, Riss and Würm of the Alpine sequence. There were probably earlier phases but the later ones tended to obliterate them. Interspersed between these glacial phases were spans when the climate ameliorated (interglacials) and similar intervals are now known to have occurred during some of the glacial phases (interstadials).

It is assumed that if the habitats of the present-day fauna are similar to those of their prehistoric ancestors then the identification of animal remains from an archaeological layer can indicate the environmental conditions pertaining at that time. Many of the animal bones excavated by archaeologists are the food remains of earlier people. Thus it must be borne in mind that they could have sought certain animals in preference to others. In the case of the palaeolithic hunters, a wide variety of animals was caught (see below, Swanscombe and Torenewton).

Small mammals, especially rodents such as voles, mice and lemmings, have been cited as being particularly important as environmental indicators since they have undergone a rapid evolution. The Pennsylvanian vole *(Microtus pennsylvanicus)* has an amazing fecundity, one female being capable of giving birth to approximately one hundred young a year. Also small mammals are more susceptible than large mammals to alterations in the local environment.

However, great care must be exercised in using rodents in this way since the exact causes of their present range of distribution are unknown. Some of the mechanisms underlying their distribution are the effects of predators, food requirements, competition with other species and presence of adequate shelter. Also the ancestor species may have had a different adaptability, been more plentiful and invaded more diverse areas.

One species possibly introduced by man to Orkney during prehistoric times is the Orkney vole *(Microtus arvalis)*, which still inhabits the islands today. Skeletal remains were found at Midhowe, in a chambered tomb, and the species is thought to have arrived there about 2000 BC. It is common in Europe but does not occur elsewhere in Britain except in Guernsey. On genetical grounds it is claimed that this vole's closest relatives are in Yugoslavia.

A classic excavation that illustrates environmental interpreta-

Plate 2. Mammoth tusk from Wouldham, Kent. Distance between tusk tip and broken end is 1.35 metres (4 feet 5 inches).

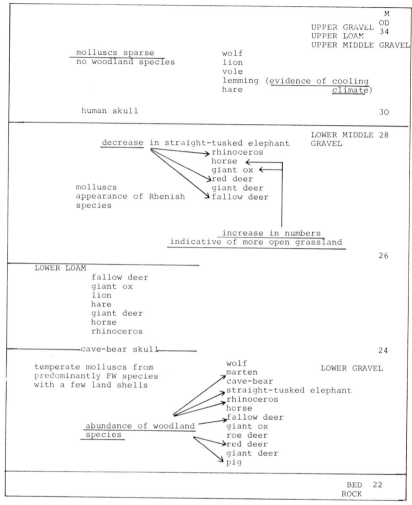

Fig. 2. Swanscombe, Kent. Stratigraphical distribution and relative abundance of the mammalian and molluscan fauna in the Barnfield gravel pit.

Plate 3. Giant Irish deer skull and antlers. Span between antler tips is 3 metres (9 feet 10 inches).

tion is the Lower Palaeolithic Barnfield gravel pit at Swanscombe, Kent. This site is 20 miles (32 km) downstream from London and the three human skull fragments discovered there are the earliest physical remains of man to have been found in Britain (fig. 2). The bone has been dated by the uranium/thorium method to 250,000 years bp but the results need to be substantiated. However, most of the material belongs to the Hoxnian interglacial (fig. 1). Species found at Swanscombe and now extinct included the cave bear *(Ursus spelaeus)*, which was represented by an almost complete skull from the sand between the Lower Gravel and the Lower Loam; wolf *(Canis lupus)*; straight-tusked elephant *(Palaeoloxodon antiquus)*; two species of rhinoceros *(Dicerorhinus kirchbergensis* and *Dicerorhinus hemitoechus)*; giant ox *(Bos primigenius)*; lion *(Panthera leo)* and giant deer *(Megaceros* species). Plate 3 shows the skull and spectacular antlers of a giant Irish deer.

The mammals from the lower deposits — roe deer, fallow deer, lion, wolf, giant deer, hare, red deer, pig, ox, marten and horse — suggest a temperate climate. It is claimed that the site was probably surrounded by woodland since the pig, marten and deer are woodland species. Further, the middle deposits showed an increase in horse and giant ox together with a decrease of elephant, perhaps indicating a more open environment. However, the number of fragments on which these ideas are based is not very large. Further up in the sequence a few voles were found, as

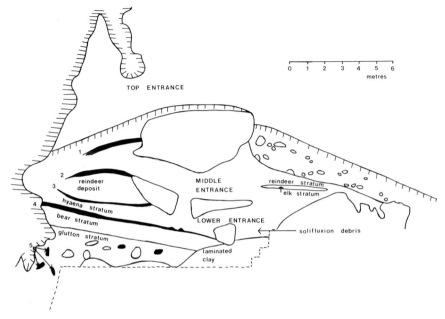

Fig. 3. Torenewton Cave, Torbryan, South Devon. Section through the deposits (after Sutcliffe and Zeuner, 1962). Numbers 1 to 5 refer to the stalagmite layers within the cave.

well as the remains of a lemming, which enjoys steppe or tundra conditions. Well preserved molluscs were also found at the site and the occurrence of different species according to climatic factors reinforced the information already divulged by the mammal bones (fig. 2).

As well as by the skull fragments, man's presence is denoted by the remains of flint tools which would have been useful for butchering the animals.

While Lower Palaeolithic British man chose sites which occurred mainly on river terraces in deposits of gravel, sand and loam, Upper Palaeolithic man generally inhabited caves. One example is Torenewton Cave in South Devon (fig. 3). Animal remains in the lower layers of the cave included the brown bear *(Ursus arctos)*, wolf *(Canis lupus)*, fox *(Vulpes vulpes)* and lion *(Panthera leo)*. Remains of the glutton *(Gulo gulo)*, horse *(Equus caballus)*, reindeer *(Rangifer tarandus)* and hare *(Lepus* species) occurred while the rhinoceros, *Coelodonta* species and bovine remains were rare. The fauna represents a cold climate. Above these layers, further up in the stratigraphy was an enormous deposit of hyena bones *(Crocuta crocuta)*. So far thirteen hundred isolated hyena teeth have been excavated by Dr A. J. Sutcliffe and Dr F. E. Zeuner and these represented at least seventy-six adult and forty-one juvenile animals. The number could be increased since it is known that a previous excavation uncovered many teeth but their whereabouts are now uncertain.

It would seem that at this time the cave was being used as a den by hyenas and not inhabited by man. A large number of coprolites (see chapter 9) were also found. A few remains of wolf *(Canis lupus)*, fox *(Vulpes vulpes)*, lion *(Panthera leo)*, rhinoceros *(Dicerorhinus hemitoechus)*, hippopotamus *(Hippopotamus amphibius)*, fallow deer *(Dama* species), red deer *(Cervus elaphus)* and hare *(Lepus* species) indicate a warmer climate, possibly an interglacial. These animals were probably carried into the cave by the hyenas.

Outside the cave a layer of elk bones was uncovered and above this a layer of reindeer bones together with a great many antlers which had been collected by humans. There were over four hundred fragments of mainly shed antlers but only seventeen teeth and bone fragments. Since reindeer is the only animal to occur in any quantity it would appear that the climate had deteriorated. Further, when the shed antler fragments were measured it was found that they could only have belonged to young or female deer, not adult males. As present-day females and young animals shed their antlers between late spring and early summer and bucks shed their antlers between November and March it could be assumed that the cave was occupied from the end of March into summer but not during autumn or winter. An alternative theory could be that the shed reindeer antler had been collected and stored over a long period of time. Reindeer antler was one of the most important raw materials used by Upper Palaeolithic man. These particular reindeer antlers had been worked by humans since only the bases and fragments of irregular shape were left, there being no straight portions of beam.

Although many species, for example mammoth, woolly rhinoceros, cave bear, cave lion, bison, hyena, arctic fox, giant deer and reindeer, certainly did not survive the end of the last glacial period in Britain, the reason for their disappearance is less clear. In the post-glacial period the temperature rose and tree cover spread, so the habitats of species like the giant deer and reindeer were severely affected. Woodland species such as the aurochs, wild boar, elk and red and roe deer increased because they were more suited to this environment. However, even with the increased temperature, rhinoceros, hippopotamus and lion did not reappear in Britain and this fact and the absence of the mammoth, woolly rhinoceros, cave bear and others have been linked to man's effect as a hunter.

The archetypal site of the early mesolithic is Star Carr, in the Vale of Pickering, north-east Yorkshire, where Professor J. G. D. Clark excavated a rich deposit of organic matter between 1949 and 1953. Star Carr was essentially a post-glacial hunter-gatherer camp site of the eighth millennium BC, situated in a lakeside environment. The faunal material is under review in order to determine during which seasons the site was occupied.

The original interpretation of the site as a winter base camp depended on the finding of a high proportion of unshed red deer antler, i.e. sixty-five out of one hundred and six antlers. The shed antler suggested occupation of the site into early April, when antlers were discarded by the deer. The occurrence of large numbers of unshed roe deer antlers was thought to support occupation in April since the deer do not discard their velvet until early in that month. Nearly half the elk antlers recovered had been broken from the skull, indicating that occupation had begun before early January, since elk normally lose their antlers then. Occupation as early as October was eliminated since roe deer discard their antlers at that time of year and there were no signs of any shed antler. So on these premises Professor J. G. D. Clark proposed that the site had been occupied for only five months of the year.

However, the occurrence of crane and possibly stork bones argues against this, both species being summer visitors. Also, it is likely that the unshed antlers of roe deer indicate summer occupation since roe deer antlers could have been acquired from late summer to April. The presence of young red deer and elk supports this. Further, shed red deer antlers could have been collected and stored so their presence on the site may be unrelated to season. The unshed deer antler could equally well have belonged to animals during the summer. In conclusion, it appears from the faunal remains that there is stronger evidence for a summer occupation.

One of the most interesting finds from Star Carr was a series of stag frontlets (plate 4) with parts of the antlers still in place. The antlers had been reduced in girth in order to reduce weight while retaining the profile. The interior of the frontal part of the skull

Plate 4. Star Carr stag frontlet. (Copyright: British Museum.)

had been shaped in such a way as to reduce the sharp features, and the parietal bones had been perforated. Professor Clark interpreted the objects as masks and suggested that they could have been used for stalking, for attracting the attention of deer or for ceremonial activities such as dances connected with the increase or well-being of these animals.

Domestication

The earliest evidence for animal domestication in Britain comes from Star Carr in the eighth millennium BC, where cranial and jawbone fragments were identified as belonging to domestic dog. Domesticated dogs have been found in palaeolithic contexts from other parts of the world, e.g. Palegawra, Iraq, *c* 12,000 years bp. The criteria used for determining domestication include reduction of jawbone size and the spaces between individual teeth.

It is claimed that the earliest radiocarbon dates for the occurrence of domesticated pigs and cattle come from Greece. Sheep/goats were probably first domesticated in the Near East. Domesticated cattle are known to have descended from the wild species *Bos primigenius. Bos primigenius* was indigenous to the British Isles but whether it became domesticated in the British Isles is a moot point (fig. 4). Certainly neolithic colonisers brought domesticated sheep/goats and they could have conveyed

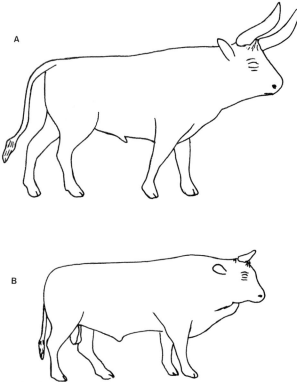

Fig. 4. Distinction in size between wild and modern domesticated cattle. **A** The wild ox *(Bos primigenius)*. Ranged in height from *c* 1500 to 1750 millimetres (4 feet 11 inches to 5 feet 9 inches). **B** A present-day domestic steer.

cattle as well. Transport of immature animals would have presented less of a problem on board the boats. The horse existed in small numbers during the mesolithic, early neolithic and bronze ages and it was probably domesticated during the bronze age.

Distinctions between early wild and domestic species have not been satisfactorily resolved since morphological changes are not easy to detect. An examination of the bone microstructure was thought to be a valid way of differentiating between species. Thin sections of bone were viewed under cross-polarised light but the results so far have proved inconclusive.

The most reliable method at present is to view the age and sex structures of the animal bone samples under consideration. In hunting economies there is a deliberate trend to avoid juvenile game even though young animals are more vulnerable. Instead, the adult animals are sought since they yield a much higher percentage of meat and the younger members are preserved, thus conserving the stock. High percentages of slaughtered immature animals have been proposed as evidence of domesticated species.

Sheep and goats were not indigenous to Britain and the domesticated species arrived with the neolithic settlers. Neolithic sheep were small and slender-limbed, rather like a Soay sheep (plate 5). It is extremely difficult to distinguish sheep bones from goat bones and the best way is to use the skull and horn cores. A complete goat skeleton was excavated from the neolithic site of Windmill Hill, Wiltshire. Domestic cattle are also found on neolithic sites but were small compared with the wild aurochsen; however, they were larger than those of the succeeding bronze age. Pigs were also small and had an elongated snout.

From the neolithic period onwards an increasing use was made of domesticated animals and the proportion of wild animals found on archaeological sites decreases dramatically. The use of these mammal bones for environmental reconstruction is thus minimal and other lines of evidence are used, for example molluscs and insects.

Plate 5. Soay sheep. (Reproduced by courtesy of Professor P. Jewell.)

Quantification

A question of immediate importance to archaeologists is how many animals of each species are represented on an archaeological site. This information can give ideas about the availability and abundance of animals for eating and also, as has already been seen, descriptions of the environment.

In the past the analysis of palaeolithic bone samples has concentrated on the identification of species. For later deposits of bone, from the neolithic to medieval periods, estimates of species abundance have been calculated by two main methods: number of bone fragments, and minimum number of animals (MIN).

There are many variables affecting the recovery of bone fragments from the earth and these include: weathering; poor retrieval by the excavator; physical and chemical composition of bone — some bones are more robust than others and therefore preserve better, e.g. pig jawbones, while immature bones do not preserve as well as mature ones; butchery practices (see below); cooking processes — heavily boiled and roasted bone loses much of its organic matter and so becomes brittle and breaks more easily than fresh bone when buried; taphonomy (see Glossary); soil acidity — in certain geographical areas the soils are too acid for bone preservation to occur; climate; selective retrieval by the modern excavator of larger bones as opposed to smaller ones; extraction of bone by early man for tools and ornaments — these bones, e.g. metapodials, tend to be missing from refuse deposits.

The number of bone fragments method is the oldest method and is the only way early bone reports can be compared. The method entails simply counting the number of bone fragments belonging to each species. Only bone fragments with old breaks should be counted; recent breakage is easy to detect as the bone appears fresh. Mammal bone identification manuals are listed in chapter 12 but there is really no substitute for a reference collection of skeletons (Cornwall 1956; Ryder 1968; Schmid 1972).

A problem with this method is that one can never be sure of the independence of bone fragments from each other. An analysis of the way a bone has been butchered can help to shed light on this difficulty. For example, if cow femurs are smashed into small fragments on one site and on another site are left whole, the calculation based on the number of bone fragments per species could be greatly distorted when the two sites are compared. In order partially to overcome this, only bone fragments which have some diagnostic feature, for instance proximal and distal epi-

Plate 6. Butchered cattle shoulder blades from Romano-British Colchester. In order to sever the shoulder joints, chops were made through the supraglenoid tubercles. The holes in the blades suggest that the joints had been hung up, possibly for smoking.

physes or fragments with foramina, are counted. Plate 6 shows butchered animal bone from Roman Colchester. Another drawback of counting the number of bone fragments, but one which can be compensated for, is that different species have different numbers of bones in their skeletons; for example a dog has fifty-two phalanges, a pig forty-eight, a cow twenty-four and a horse twelve.

Palaeontologists used the MIN method in the 1920s and 1930s. It was later introduced into American archaeology in the 1950s. There are three main methods of calculating MIN:

(A) The skeletal part of the species most numerous in the sample is counted: for example, a bone deposit consists of thirteen right cow humeri, ten left cow humeri, twelve right cow radii and eight left cow radii. It could be stated that a minimum number of thirteen animals is present. However, the ten left humeri might not be associated with the thirteen right humeri and thus there could be a minimum number of twenty-three animals present. Method B provides greater accuracy.

(B) Dr R. Chaplin, in his book *The Study of Bone from Archaeological Sites,* describes how each bone can be carefully analysed and matched to others of the same sort with respect to age, sex and size.

$$\text{GMT} = C_i^t/2 + D^t$$

GMT = grand minimum number of animals represented.
C_i^t = total number of comparable paired elements.
D^t = total number of dissimilar elements.

(C) The eruption and wear pattern of the teeth make it possible to decide in a large number of cases whether the mandibles are from the same individual or not.

Method A tends to over-represent species with small numbers, B tries to avoid this and C tries to combine A and B.

Although the MIN method is the more popular method in use, Grayson in his paper 'Minimum Numbers and Sample Size in Vertebrate Faunal Analysis' has pointed out that MIN varies greatly according to whether site stratigraphy is used, i.e. the maximum distinction method, or is not used, i.e. the minimum distinction method. Fig. 5 illustrates the differences that can arise if stratigraphy is or is not used. Unfortunately researchers invariably do not state how they have derived the MIN quantity.

The number of bone fragments per species or the minimum number of animals per species can be expressed in percentage form; however, in the case of MIN it is impossible to calculate percentages that have any statistical significance. Payne, 'On the Interpretation of Bone Samples from Archaeological Sites', has demonstrated that the relative frequency of pig, sheep/goat and cow at Lerna 2 and 3 in two different samples was significantly different at the 1 per cent level using the number of bone fragments but in terms of MIN the samples were not significantly different at the 10 per cent level. Lerna is a neolithic and bronze age site in Greece. The difficulty in the statistical treatment was caused by simple inflation: a few animals may be represented by a large number of identified specimens. MIN obviously exaggerates the importance of the rarer animals.

It has been assumed that, with a reasonable sample size, and when all the variables affecting calculation of MIN and the number of bone fragments have been weighted for, the two methods should give similar results. A number of researchers have compared these quantitative measures and pointed out the

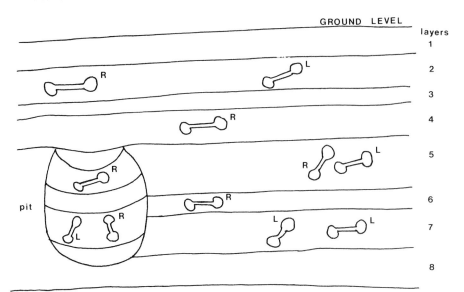

Fig. 5. Calculation of minimum number of animals (MIN). This is a vertical section of a Roman dwelling site. For the sake of simplicity the bone represents a cow humerus and R and L correspond to the right and left elements respectively. The numbers 1 to 8 refer to the site layers, the oldest in age being layer 8 and the youngest layer 1. **A** *Minimum distinction method* (without stratigraphy). Assuming that all the layers and the pit are of the same date, then six cows may be represented. **B** *Maximum distinction method* (with stratigraphy). Sometimes there is no way of knowing whether the animal remains among the layers are related to each other. If we assume that they are not related to each other and each layer and pit layer is a separate entity then only eight animals may be represented.

inherent difficulties in using them. It has been shown graphically that there is a parabolic curve relationship between MIN plotted against the number of bone fragments (fig. 6). Grayson has shown that one can determine a lower limit for MIN and the number of bone fragments below which comparisons between the two are not viable.

It has been claimed that the MIN method is not of great value in urban conditions where retail butchery may have been practised. It is possible neither to distinguish animals represented by joints rather than carcasses nor to know whether some animals have been collected for industrial purposes; for example, a large number of cattle horn cores and phalanges could be indicative of a tannery.

Both methods are of value and can act as a check on each other, particularly if estimates are made concerning each bone of

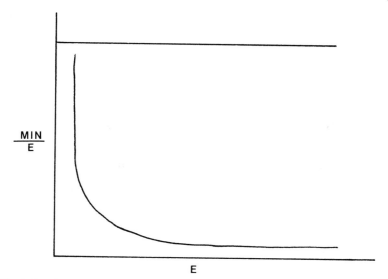

Fig. 6. Graph showing the relationship between the minimum number of animals (MIN) and the number of bone fragments (E).

a species skeleton; for example, the scapulae of a cow could be represented by four hundred recognisable bone fragments and a minimum number of animals of two hundred. The lower value for MIN occurs because the bones have been sorted into right and left elements. The occurrence of different sorts of skeletal elements gives evidence of whether the bones represent actual food refuse or waste and offal from butchery. Scapulae, humeri and femora are all meat-bearing bones while phalanges and skull fragments do not bear meat.

The classical Roman author Columella relates that having killed a pig when it is thirsty one should bone it thoroughly since this makes the salted flesh less oily and causes it to keep better (Columella xll, 55). This could account for the pig's apparent scarcity on some Roman sites.

In any consideration of diet it would be much more useful to think in terms of meat potential than percentages of bone fragments or MIN. However, although various methods have been proposed, there is still no precise way of determining the body weights of domestic animals from the bone remains. A relative assessment of the meat contribution from a site can be gained by multiplying MIN or the number of bone fragments by the following factors and expressing the numbers as percentages:

cow 408 kilograms (900 pounds); horse 363 kilograms (800 pounds); sheep 56.7 kilograms (125 pounds); pig 90.7 kilograms (200 pounds). These figures are the average carcass weights.

Aging

Aging in this context means the determination of an animal's life span, that is the age at which it died. Accurate aging can give information not only on human dietary preferences but also the age at which animals were slaughtered and even their season of death. Further data can be obtained concerning the age structure of the flock or herd which in turn would reflect their economic status, but great care is needed in making any interpretations since the evidence in many cases consists of food refuse, and man may have been selective in his choice.

There are four main methods of estimating the age of an animal: (A) eruption of the teeth; (B) dentine and enamel wear patterns of the teeth; (C) measurement of tooth height; (D) fusion of the long bone epiphyses.

In his paper on aging in Brothwell and Higgs's book *Science in Archaeology*, Silver gives two sets of teeth eruption dates for the domesticated farm animals, cattle, sheep and pigs. One set consists of modern figures for improved breeds and the other of data from eighteenth and nineteenth-century animals. It was thought that late eruption dates were characteristic of these earlier animals. There is much concern about the use of modern or old aging data since the economic interpretations can be quite different. For reasons given below, modern aging data appear more appropriate.

The sequence of tooth eruption is not affected by the environment or nutrition. A sheep/goat has three lower and upper premolars and three lower and upper molars. For sheep, the modern sequence is that the second and third premolars erupt together followed by the fourth premolar whereas in the iron age the third and fourth premolars erupted together followed by the second premolar. It has been suggested that since the sequence of eruption was probably controlled by genetic factors, then sequential differences in various groups could be regarded as by-products of selective breeding. Also these traits could be changed by geographical movements of animals.

In certain iron age sheep mandibles osteologists have noted that the crypt for the third molar is visible in the mandible by the time the second molar comes into wear. However, Silver gives a period of about two years between the eruption dates of these

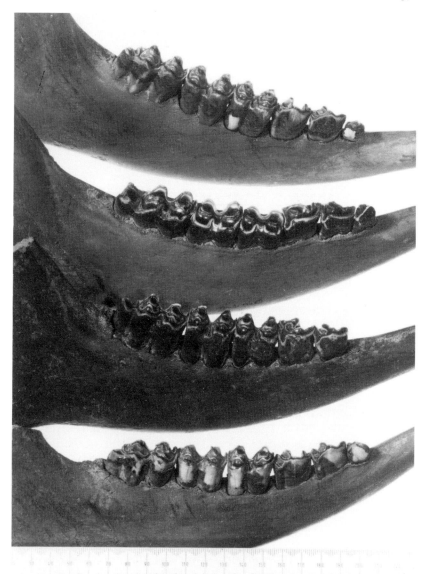

Plate 7. Cattle mandibles from Romano-British Colchester. Each mandible has a set of six teeth, three premolars and three molars (except the third jaw from the top, where the first premolar is broken). All the teeth have been worn down, exposing dentine with islands of enamel.

two teeth in semi-wild hill sheep. The question thus arises: how accurate are these old aging figures? In 1927 Professor Sir George T. Brown wrote in his book *Dentition as Indicative of the Age of the Animals of the Farm* that the original version of the development of the teeth was based on imperfect observation or on the custom of one writer quoting in good faith from another.

Professor Brown questioned the late eruption dates of earlier authors since from 1850 to 1902, with intensive breeding, no change was seen in the dates. Professor Brown set down the rules governing age and dentition for the Royal Smithfield Show, which remained unchanged from 1889 until 1975.

Grant and Payne have developed methods for recording the tooth wear patterns of sheep/goats. Grant has also recorded the wear patterns of teeth for pigs and cattle. As a tooth wears down, the enamel and dentine form different patterns; groups of animals can be isolated that fit a particular pattern (plate 7). However, tooth wear is dependent on factors that differ between sites, and so it can only give information concerning age groups in one population.

Measurement of tooth height was rejected by Severinghaus when he worked on white-tailed deer, since individual variation in tooth size was sufficient to preclude the use of any such measurements for constructing age spans.

The method of epiphysial fusion is not an absolutely reliable technique, as Watson has shown. He emphasised that problems arise when a range is treated as if it were a point: for example, the distal epiphysis of a sheep metacarpal fuses between eighteen and twenty-four months. In considering a sample of sheep metacarpals 40 per cent of which are fused, one could say that 40 per cent of sheep died at over eighteen to twenty-four months. But Watson corrects this by stating that any fused bone must be from an individual that died at over eighteeen months but is not necessarily from an individual that died at over twenty-four months. Any unfused bone must be from an individual that died at under twenty-four months but is not necessarily from an individual that died at under eighteen months (plate 8).

There are clearly many difficulties in using these methods. A large number of variables affect tooth eruption and wear ages. If warranted, a more time-consuming method may be applied, for instance thin sectioning the secondary dental cementum of teeth in order to count the growth rings. It has been claimed that this method can age any ovine species to within three to six months.

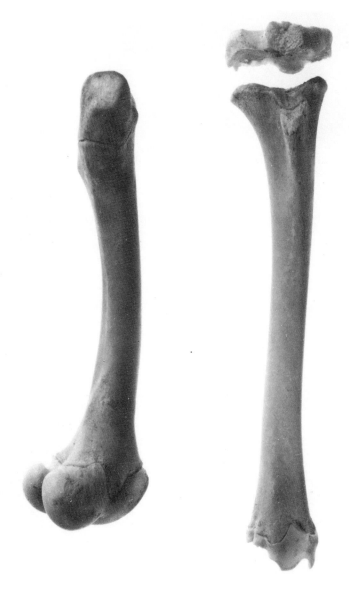

Plate 8. Sheep femur (left) and tibia epiphyses. The proximal epiphysis of the tibia has not fused. The remaining epiphyses have fused fairly recently, the epiphysial fusion lines being apparent.

Sexing

Information concerning human diet, animal husbandry and industries, such as horn, hide, wool and glue, can be enhanced by a knowledge of sexing. The sexing of animal bones is not always clear-cut and it is recommended that reliance should not be placed on a single method. As many different methods as possible should be used, each acting as a check on the others. For instance, in sexing cattle bones extreme examples of bulls and females can be identified from the metacarpal bones (fig. 7). However, small bulls and large females from several intermixed breeds can cloud the picture and castrated animals can cause further complications.

Professor Charles Higham has made an important contribution to faunal studies in his investigation of Aberdeen Angus and Red Danish cattle. By using modern data, he has demonstrated statistically that the sexes of cattle breeds can be separated metrically. The principal assumption in Higham's work is that if for any given modern bone sexual dimorphism is established then it will be assumed that quantitatively similar dimorphism was displayed by the same bone dimension in prehistoric animals of the same species. He found that some bone dimensions showed high degrees of sexual dimorphism, e.g. metacarpal distal width, while others displayed little, e.g. astragalus length. Further, measurements of length appeared less sexually dimorphic than those of breadth and bones of the fore limb showed more sexual dimorphism than those of the hind limb. Bones showing the most marked sexual dimorphism were the metacarpal, radius and mandible, including dentition. The low degree of overlap between cow, steer and bull metacarpals on the basis of proximal and distal width-to-length ratios enabled most complete metacarpals (from animals of the same breed) to be separated into cows, bulls and steers. With a statistical test Higham proved that a sample of fifteen to twenty specimens is all that is needed to provide an accurate estimate of the population mean and variance. Fig. 7 shows how to take measurements on cattle metapodials in order to determine sex.

Howard measured 136 metapodials from recent cattle, breed unspecified, and constructed two indices which she maintained were reasonably constant within each sex. Further, she stated that despite alterations in the absolute size the relative proportions of the bones had not changed with time to any great extent, an important implication for archaeological material. Although these dimensions have a limited discriminatory value they do

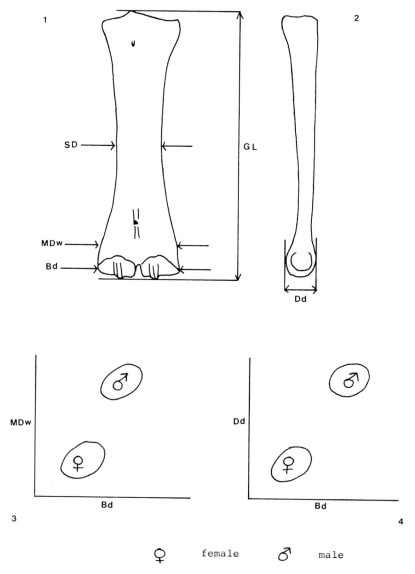

Fig. 7. A demonstration of cattle metacarpal measurements in order to determine sex. **1:** Anterior aspect of metacarpal bone: GL, greatest length; SD, minimum shaft width; MDw, maximum distal diaphysial width; Bd, maximum distal width. **2:** Lateral aspect of metacarpal bone: Dd, maximum distal thickness. **3** and **4:** the above measurements plotted graphically after Higham, 1969, showing a sexual separation.

provide a useful check on some of Higham's methods.

In my book *Zooarchaeology, A Study of the Roman North-western Provinces* I describe in detail the problems of cattle sexing at Sheepen and also several other sites of the Romano-British period in Essex. Both the Higham and Howard methods led me to suspect that many female cattle were present. However, I could not state this conclusively so I looked for other evidence and found it in the morphology of the pelvic girdle. In female cattle the ilio-pectineal process is flattened and tends to be pointed forward. It is connected with a concave depression under the acetabulum which exhibits a shallow medial rim. The pubic bone in cross-section is lozenge or diamond-shaped. In male cattle the pubis and medial acetabulum rim are much thicker with no concave depression under the acetabulum; the pubis tends to be more oval. This gave the supporting evidence needed, a ratio of nineteen females to two males.

Cattle horn cores were scarce at Sheepen, which was unfortunate since an examination of these bones can give a good idea of sex. The shape, size and porosity of the bone are the main determinants, after the method of Dr Armitage and Dr Clutton-Brock (plate 9).

Sexing of sheep/goat long bones remains a problem since differentiation of the two species is not always easy. Also it has been found that measurements of male and female animals tend to overlap. Horn cores are of more use in this direction. Sexing by the mandibular canine is a useful method for pigs since male canines are larger than female canines and they also have open roots.

Metrication

Perhaps the most intriguing question concerning prehistoric and historic animals is what did they look like. A thorough metrical analysis can provide the basis for an investigation but too often, certainly in the pre-Roman iron age and Romano-British periods, researchers have not taken the relevant measurements. It is important to estimate the build of an animal, whether it is gracile or robust, and so long-bone mid-shaft, medio-lateral and antero-posterior width dimensions should be recorded. Further, with the horse, measurements of the mid-shaft circumference are necessary. A good comparative knowledge of anatomy is helpful in order to determine muscular insertions and such like. Also length ratios of the upper limb to lower limb bones of the hind and fore legs are vital pieces of data to assimilate into any

Plate 9. Romano-British cattle horn cores from Sheepen, Essex.

Plate 10. Wooden model of spotted Egyptian oxen ploughing, 2000 BC. (Copyright: British Museum.)

reconstruction of the animal. In addition questions of sex and age should be considered. Whole skeletons are of great value in any re-creation, since horn core and pelvic girdle features can determine sex and also act as a check on each other. Dr A. v. d. Driesch has written a book describing how to measure domestic mammal and bird bones.

Metrical data do have their limitations for they cannot describe the colour or type of coat belonging to an animal. Thus other lines of evidence must be investigated, for example plate 10, which shows spotted Egyptian oxen ploughing *c* 2000 BC.

The earliest traces of artistic ability are expressed in the cave art of the palaeolithic ice age hunters. The caves are found mainly in the south-west of France and northern Spain. A variety of animals are depicted on the cave walls, the more common being horse, bison, wild ox and red deer, together with giant deer, ibex, musk-ox, cave lion, bear and mammoth. Surprisingly no serious study has been made of these paintings by a zoologist. This is unfortunate since so many fanciful notions have been advanced for the art. In north-west Europe representations are rare in prehistoric art until the iron age and Roman periods.

Professor P. Jewell has demonstrated that there was a diminution in size of cattle from the neolithic to the pre-Roman

Plate 11. *Bos primigenius* skull, from Lowes Farm, Littleport, Cambridgeshire. (Copyright: Faculty of Archaeology and Anthropology, Cambridge University.)

iron age; in the Roman period larger animals existed but there was no overall improvement in their size. Plate 11 shows a skull of *Bos primigenius* (the ancestor of domestic cattle), which was excavated at Lowes Farm near Littleport (Cambridgeshire) and was dated 1390 bc by radiocarbon dating. The post-cranial skeleton was also recovered from the bronze age peat, as is shown in plate 12, and the animal was found to be a bull. *Bos primigenius* became extinct in the seventeenth century, the last animal being killed in Poland. In Britain the species survived until the bronze age.

The Celtic shorthorn ox, *Bos longifrons,* originated on bronze age sites, and many Roman settlements exhibited this type of animal together with the larger variety. Present-day Kerry cattle are the nearest equivalent to these beasts. Hornless or polled cattle first appeared on iron age sites, e.g. All Cannings Cross (Wiltshire).

There was also a reduction in the size of some wild animals in post-glacial Britain, for example red deer. This is associated with the change from a woodland to a hill habitat brought about by human activity.

The present-day Soay sheep from St Kilda represent feral animals which were the domesticated sheep of the neolithic and later periods (plate 5). The sheep are characterised by a short tail, long slender legs and pigmented coat. Noddle has demonstrated that the scapulae of short-tailed breeds, such as the Soay, have comparatively longer necks than those of the long-tailed breeds, while crossbreeds fall in between (fig. 8).

The scapulae of sheep/goats from first-century Sheepen were measured by the author, i.e. the width of the scapula neck (SLC after v.d. Driesch) and the minimum length of the neck (ASG, fig. 8). When the ratio of these measurements was considered they did not coincide with measurements Noddle provided for Soay sheep and domestic goats. However, they did coincide with measurements for the long-tailed Clun Forest breed. Thus it was thought reasonable to assume that long-tailed sheep were present in first-century Roman Britain. Further, Dr M. Ryder's work on ancient skin remains supports this conclusion (see chapter 8). Fig. 9 illustrates a long-tailed sheep from Autun, France, dated to the

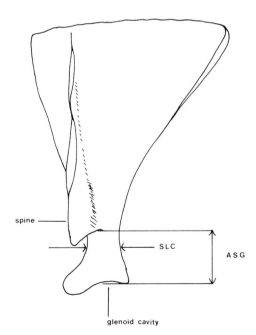

Fig. 8. An illustration of sheep/goat measurements to determine scapula shape. ASG: length of scapula neck from the spine to edge of glenoid cavity. SLC: minimum width of scapula neck.

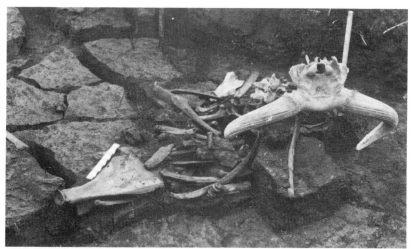

Plate 12. *Bos primigenius* skull and post-cranial skeleton excavated from the bronze age peat at Lowes Farm, Littleport, Cambridgeshire.

fifth century AD. Hornless sheep skulls have been found on a few Romano-British sites, e.g. Findon, West Sussex. A four-horned sheep skull has been excavated at Roman Colchester. Multi-horned sheep were bred at iron age Longthorpe, near Peterborough, the Roman fort of Newstead in Scotland and possibly

Fig. 9 *(left).* Sheep carving on a marble slab from Autun (Saône-et-Loire). Dated fifth century AD. (Musée Rollin, Autun.)

Fig. 10 *(right).* Bronze boar from Neuvy-en-Sullias (Loiret). Height 680 millimetres (26¾ inches); length 1260 millimetres (49½ inches); width 330 millimetres (13 inches). (Musée Historique Orléanais, Orleans.)

Plate 13. Modern (centre) and Romano-British sheep skulls from Chelmsford, Essex. Viewed from behind.
Plate 14. Romano-British dog bones from Colchester. The remains of four dogs are represented by four pairs of tibiae. Note the shorter curved long bones immediately to the top and bottom left of the plate.

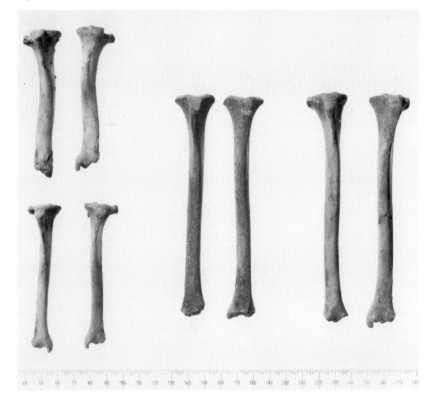

Plate 15. Medieval cat skulls from Colchester, Essex. Frontal view.

bronze age Jahrlshof in Shetland. Plate 13 shows a modern Soay sheep skull compared with some Romano-British remains from Chelmsford, Essex.

In the case of horses, there has been insufficient research carried out concerning the effects of gelding on bone structure, although it is known that taller animals result. Roman literature, sculpture and epigraphy point to the abundant use of mules in the Empire. Unfortunately, although asses can be distinguished from horses with reasonable ease, the identification of mules presents problems.

During the iron age immature boar's meat was a popular dish, thus there are very few bones available for measurement since the epiphyses had not fused. However, there are several sculptures of boars, such as the carving of a boar on a stone sculpture of the boar-god at Euffigneix, France, and the bronze statue of a boar from Neuvy-en-Sullias, Loiret, France. Fig. 10 shows the characteristically long-legged beast.

An interesting collection of dog bones can be seen in plate 14, which demonstrates the considerable variation in shape and size of Romano-British canines from Colchester. This is very characteristic of the Roman period, which also saw the appearance of the lap dog.

The Romans introduced the domestic cat to Britain. Very few remains of dogs and cats have been found, except at Portchester (Hampshire), where there was a high proportion of both dogs and cats. This suggests that on many sites the animals were accorded separate burial. Plate 15 shows some medieval cat skulls from Colchester. The skulls were found buried in a cesspit together with their post-cranial skeletons; altogether nine individuals were represented. This method of disposal was quite common in the medieval period.

3
Birds

The avian remains recovered from archaeological sites mainly consist of bone but in certain circumstances feathers, claws, beaks, skin, droppings, egg shells and mummies may be found. In Britain there has been a sad neglect of this type of faunal study. Most bird reports constitute lists of species and hardly any attempt has been made to integrate this information into the main excavation report. The identification of species can be extremely tedious and difficult since the bones of many birds resemble each other quite closely. Also there is scant data concerning metrical analyses. Linked with the difficulties of identification is the lack, as with fish, of reliable skeletal guides to species. Inefficient sampling from sites caused by lack of sieving may be another factor contributing to the sparsity of reports. However, avian osteology is a field that could be exploited by the enthusiastic amateur providing he or she is prepared to build up a comparative collection of bird skeletons. Dr R. Chaplin explains how to undertake this procedure in his book *The Study of Bone from Archaeological Sites*.

The identification of bird bones can enlighten the archaeologist on diet, environment, social customs, climate and seasonal information. Birds inhabit a wide range of environment but for simplicity they will be considered under two headings, domesticated and wild.

The Heuneburg iron age hillfort in Bavaria, Germany, provided the oldest known remains of domestic fowl from Europe. The species was introduced into Britain during the pre-Roman iron age and occurred at *Camulodunum* (Colchester, Essex), Kingsdown Camp (Mells, Somerset), Slonk Hill (Sussex), Gussage All Saints (Dorset), Skeleton Green (Braughing, Hertfordshire), Winklebury (Wiltshire) and Bishopstone (Sussex). Julius Caesar comments that the Britons did not eat fowls, hares or geese. They were kept as pets (*BG* xii, 16).

Castration of fowls was practised by the Romans. Varro relates that the operation involved the burning of the leg spurs with red-hot irons, the wounds being healed with clay (*De Re Rustica* iii, 9). This surely was an additional undertaking to that of castration; the removal of the spurs would have reduced the fighting ability of the bird. The operation could have deformed the underlying bony part but the author has found no evidence of

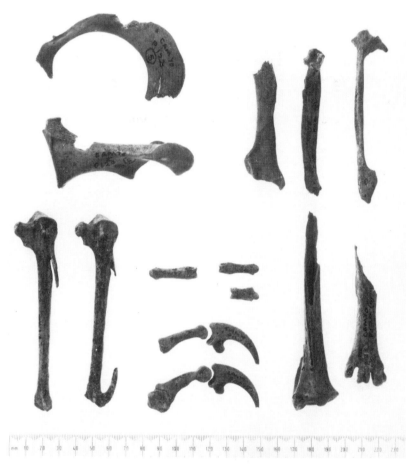

Plate 16. White-tailed eagle remains *(Haliaeetus albicilla)*, first century AD. Found in a rubbish pit at Sheepen, Essex.

this in any of the archaeological bone she has examined so far.

In the Romano-British period domestic fowl dominates most sites if one counts the number of bone fragments. Fowls were bred not only for eating but also for cock fighting, as Columella describes heavy bets being made in the middle of the first century AD (Columella viii, 12). Geese are found rarely and are thought to have been introduced by the Romans. Mallard are more popular, although it is difficult to decide from the skeletal remains whether the species is domesticated or wild.

The occurrence of whole raven skeletons suggests that the birds may have been kept as pets in Roman Britain.

Bird bones found at first-century Sheepen, Essex, provided evidence that the site was situated in a marshy environment with densely vegetated meadowland. An abundance of pig remains supported this conclusion. Among the birds that inhabited the region were the common crane *(Grus grus)*, which used to be common in bogs and wooded swamps but is now extinct in Britain, the wigeon *(Anas penelope)*, which is common to marshes, meadows and swamps, where it breeds, and the corn crake *(Crex crex)*, which is locally common in meadows and in fields with dense vegetation. The remains of two white-tailed eagles *(Haliaeetus albicilla)* (plate 16) occurred at Sheepen. This species is now rare in Britain.

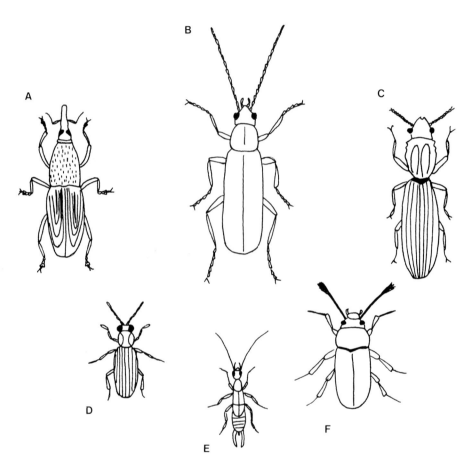

Fig. 11. Some of the insects found in the Romano-British rubbish pit at Alcester, Warwickshire. **A.** *Sitophilus granarius.* Length 3 to 4 millimetres (0.12-0.16 inch). Known as a grain weevil from earliest times; frequents foodstuffs and is injurious to wheat, corn, barley and other grains. **B.** *Rhagonycha fulva.* Length 7 to 10 millimetres (0.28-0.39 inch). Found on Umbelliferae from lowland to highland elevations of *c* 1000 metres (3300 feet). **C.** *Oryzaephilus surinamensis.* Length 2 millimetres (0.08 inch). Known as the saw-toothed grain beetle. This pest frequents meal, flour and grain of all kinds. **D.** *Anobium punctatum.* Length 3 to 5 millimetres (0.12-0.20 inch). Infests mainly timber and furniture. **E.** *Labia minor.* Length 5 to 9 millimetres (0.20-0.35 inch). A small earwig occurring in fields, meadows and forest margins. **F.** *Typhaea stercorea.* Length 2.5 to 3 millimetres (0.10-0.12 inch). Occurs on decaying vegetable matter throughout the year.

4
Insects

There are more than twenty thousand species of insects in the British Isles and, apart from the sea, they have invaded a wide range of diverse habitats. On archaeological and natural sites, anaerobic waterlogged conditions are conducive to their preservation, especially the familiar chitinous cuticle, which is particularly resistant to decay. The cuticle constitutes the exoskeleton of the insect.

Insects are very responsive to environmental change and are good climatic indicators. So far no indication of morphological evolution has been detected; all identified beetles of the late Pleistocene are referable to species still living. Also botanical evidence suggests that their environmental requirements have not significantly altered.

The identification of species is extremely time-consuming work since archaeological material is fragmentary and specimens can appear seriously distorted. Research has concentrated on the order Coleoptera, i.e. beetles, and this group covers a wide range of well defined habitats. However, there are still approximately four thousand species to become familiar with. Further, if palaeolithic samples are being analysed, then the possible number of species is increased significantly since Britain was then joined to the continent. Indeed, some insects found in interglacial deposits occur today in southern and central Europe.

Handbooks useful for identifying species are listed in chapter 12 (Joy, 1932; *Handbooks for the Identification of British Insects*, 1950). Normally insects are recovered from sites by taking 5 kilogram (11 pound) samples at 50 millimetre (2 inch) intervals vertically through the stratigraphy. Nowhere is it more clear than with insects that some deposits are more worthwhile to study than others. In any consideration of the environment, insects sampled from natural deposits are of much more use than those from archaeological deposits. Unfortunately they tend to be less common in buried soils and more profuse in town deposits. Since the Roman period, a large number of species have arrived as a result of trade. They can give information concerning living conditions, climate, food and so on but the sample to be analysed must be chosen very carefully. If this is accomplished, then data from insect studies taken in conjunction with results from other lines of research, such as pollen grains and molluscs, can be extremely informative.

For example, at Upton Warren, Derbyshire, botanical remains indicated that the Pleistocene climate had been cool, supporting willow, birch and pine trees. However, the beetles suggested a warmer climate and this evidence would seem more reliable since insects respond much more quickly to climatic events than plants. The difference in temperature between where a species is well established and its northern limits is frequently one degree Celsius, so minor climatic changes can cause dramatic expansions or contractions of an insect's habitat. In early medieval deposits from York about a dozen species of beetle occur whose northern limits are now south of Yorkshire. This could possibly be viewed as indicating a better climate in medieval times.

A good example of gleaning facts from an insect assemblage is Osborne's analysis of a Romano-British pit at Alcester, Warwickshire. He showed that the pit was a refuse pit into which had been thrown sweepings from the floor of a leather-goods factory, dung and general domestic garbage. Building timber or furniture was infested with wood-boring beetles, some of which had probably been imported. Also he proved that Roman grain stores were infested with a range of beetles including the saw-toothed grain beetle *(Oryzaephilus surinamensis)*. Some species indicated that the site was situated in open meadowland. Fig. 11 illustrates a few types of insect present.

5
Molluscs

The phylum Mollusca includes the snails, slugs, clams, oysters, octopods and nautili. As far as the archaeologist is concerned, it is more useful to group the animals according to the environment in which they are found. Thus the discussion will centre on marine and land molluscs. Not much work has been done on freshwater forms so these will be omitted here. Also, only those animals having a shell will be considered. Some of the more commonly found molluscs are shown in fig. 12. There are many identification manuals available and some are listed in chapter 12 but most of the illustrations are of adult animals and complete specimens (Shackleton, 1969; Evans, 1972; Kerney and Cameron, 1979).

Shells have been used as chronological indicators and for interpretations of climate, environment and season of site occupation. They also give evidence of diet and ornamentation. Documentary evidence from Pliny shows that the cuttlefish provided a pigment called Roman sepia for the Romans.

Samples of about 1 kilogram (2¼ pounds) size should be taken at 80 to 100 millimetre (3-4 inch) intervals vertically through the stratigraphy and wet sieved using a 0.5 millimetre mesh.

Marine molluscs

Vestiges of mesolithic man's food refuse can be seen in the vast shell middens which are found along the Atlantic seaboard, e.g. Olbylyng, 32 kilometres (20 miles) south of Copenhagen, Culver Well (Isle of Portland, Dorset) and the island of Oronsay off the west coast of Scotland. They are also found near lakes and estuaries. Although the middens are thought to contain primarily shellfish, other animals, for example fish and red deer, are found which can rival the amount of shell.

Dr P. A. Mellars painstakingly excavated six shell middens on the island of Oronsay, Scotland, which have produced a wealth of zooarchaeological data from the middle of the fourth millennium BC. Plate 17 shows a section through one of the middens. Material from the middens has been used to provide radiocarbon dates, environmental, economic and seasonal evidence. The radiocarbon dates obtained from limpet shells, retrieved from the lower levels of the Caisteal nan Gillean II midden, do not

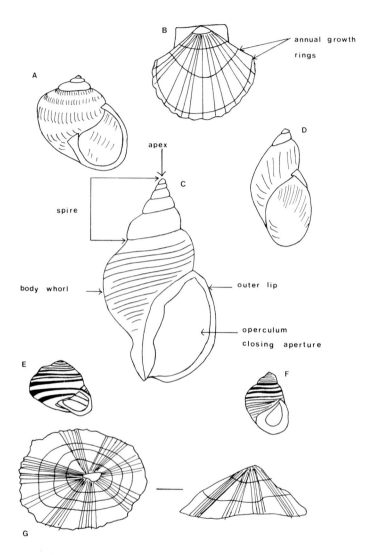

B annual growth rings

A

apex

spire

C

D

body whorl

outer lip

operculum
closing aperture

E

F

G

Fig. 12. An assortment of molluscs commonly found on archaeological sites. **A.** *Helix pomatia,* an edible land snail. **B.** *Pecten maximus,* the great scallop. Grows up to 150 millimetres (6 inches) in length and can be found offshore from low water to 60 fathoms (110 metres). **C.** *Buccinum undatum,* the common whelk. Can reach 110 millimetres (4¼ inches) in height and 65 millimetres (2½ inches) in width. Found from the shoreline down to depths of about 150 to 200 metres (490 to 650 feet). **D.** *Succinea putris,* a land snail common in marshes. Length 1.7 millimetres (0.07 inch). **E.** *Cepaea nemoralis.* Length 3 millimetres (0.12 inch). Widespread land snail found in woods, scrub and grassland. **F.** *Littorina littorea,* the periwinkle. Grows up to 30 millimetres (1.2 inches) in height. Found in the upper regions of the littoral zone. **G.** *Patella coerulea,* a very common edible species measuring 30 to 40 millimetres (1.2 to 1.6 inches) in length. Occurs in the splash zone.

Plate 17. Hearth *in situ* at base of midden deposits at Cnoc Coig, island of Oronsay, Scotland. Date *c* bc 3700/3600. (Reproduced by courtesy of Dr P. A. Mellars.)

coincide with those obtained from charcoal in the midden (plate 18).

However, the validity of radiocarbon dating marine shells is open to question. There is a tendency for the original aragonite to recrystallise into calcite, the more stable form of calcium carbonate. Thus a check must be made on the specimen by X-ray crystallography. Also the carbon in the shell carbonate is prone to exchange with non-indigenous carbon, thus the samples can be contaminated with carbon dissolved in ground water. The most recent research suggests that radiocarbon measurement of the inorganic rather than the organic fraction of shell is best. This is because the organic fraction, conchiolin, is subject to contamination by assimilation of micro-organisms. However, this does not affect carbon-14 in the carbonate fraction. The technique of amino-acid racemisation has been applied to marine shells but unlike bone there are differences in racemisation rates among different molluscan species.

Calculation of the number of shells present, whether marine or terrestrial, is accomplished by counting the apexes; thus an idea can be gained of which species are more popular in dietary terms. This is not very useful for visualising the economy of a site, so an estimate of meat weight is made. This is done by filling shells with water and measuring the volume of water. Thus it is much easier to calculate the meat weight of shellfish than that of mammals.

Measurement of shells can reveal interesting data, perhaps bearing on the time of year a site was occupied. There is a relationship between height and length of limpet shells which is determined primarily by their position in the intertidal zone. Limpets which live in the lower tidal zone are generally much flatter than ones found in the higher tidal zone. Those collected from the Oronsay midden sites had an average shell height to breadth ratio which was rather less than that of limpets collected from very low tides around the modern Oronsay coast. Dr Mellars has suggested that possibly limpets were collected almost exclusively from the lower tidal range and perhaps only during periods of spring tides.

The temperature of the water in which a shell was deposited can be obtained by the oxygen isotope technique. The principle of the method is that the ratio of oxygen isotopes deposited in the shell varies with temperature but having been deposited they remain stable. The ratio of oxygen-16 and oxygen-18 in about 0.5 milligrams of shell calcium carbonate is measured with a mass spectrometer. Also samples can be taken from seasonal layers in the shell. The use of seasonal growth lines in bivalve molluscs to determine prehistoric occupation patterns is a relatively new concept with considerable potential. Growth lines involve variations in the character of an accreting tissue in response to physiological or environmental stimuli. Thin sections are made of the shell but difficulties can be encountered in relating the growth lines to seasons (fig. 12).

Land molluscs

Land molluscs are better chronological indicators than marine species. It would clearly be advantageous if they evolved rapidly but they do not. They are probably of more importance for answering questions about local environment, although knowledge about the ecology of present-day species is incomplete. Insects can give much more detailed information concerning climate.

Dr J. G. Evans has made an enormous contribution to archaeology in his analysis of shells. In his book *The Environment of Early Man in the British Isles* he describes an ancient ploughed soil underneath a neolithic mound known as the South Street Long Barrow, Avebury (Wiltshire). This soil, 200 millimetres (8 inches) deep, contained a profusion of land snail shells. Soil samples were taken at close intervals and the shells were grouped into 'shade-loving', 'intermediate' and 'open-country' categories. The earliest fauna at South Street reflects an open, probably tundra environment without trees. Above this layer, woodland

Plate 18. Close-up of midden deposit at Caisteal nan Gillean II, island of Oronsay, Scotland. Date *c* bc 3400/3500. It shows a heavy predominance of limpets in the midden. (Reproduced by courtesy of Dr P. A. Mellars.)

species were pre-eminent and fully temperate types. Evans regarded this as the spreading of forest over Wiltshire, a result of the post-glacial climatic rise in temperature. Further up in the stratigraphy, the trees have been cleared and there are signs of plough marks.

The large snail *(Helix pomatia)* was deliberately domesticated by the Romans and introduced to Britain. The Romans bred them for such characteristics as size, colour and fecundity.

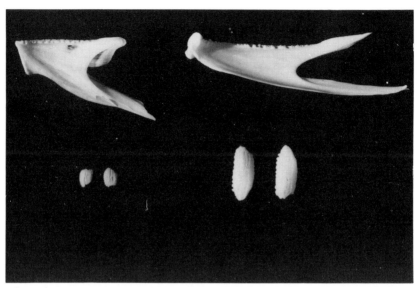

Plate 19. Fish jawbones and otoliths (inner surfaces). Left: cod *(Gadus morhua)*. Right: turbot *(Scophthalmus maximus)*.

Plate 20. Close-up view of fish jawbones showing teeth sockets. Top: turbot *(Scophthalmus maximus)*. Bottom: cod *(Gadus morhua)*.

6
Fish

An analysis of fish remains can provide information concerning human diet, climate, environment, seasonal occupation and fishing methods. As is the case with avian bone, there are no descriptive guides concerning the skeletons of north European species. Specimens must be identified with the aid of a good reference collection. Jawbones and teeth are the easiest bones to identify, i.e. the dentary and premaxillary bones. Scales and otoliths can be identified to species but are rarely found. Otoliths are composed of aragonite, the crystal form of calcium carbonate, and are found in the fish inner ear. They are concerned with the hearing and balance of fish. All the higher bony fishes have three pairs of otoliths, the sagittae, lapilli and asterisci. The sagitta is much larger than the others and the surface of its inner face allows identification to species level. Some examples of jawbones and otoliths are shown in plates 19 and 20.

In order to recover a representative sample from a site, sieving is essential. Dr A. Wheeler and A. Jones found a considerable contrast in the number of species recovered by hand picking as opposed to sieving at the medieval site of Great Yarmouth. Very few species were represented by the hand-picked material, e.g. cod and plaice, while sieved samples contained cod, thornback ray, herring, horse mackerel, whiting, haddock, plaice, flounder, sole, eel, flatfish, turbot, ling, conger and bass.

Evidence that the climate of the British Isles may have changed since neolithic times was provided by Dr Wheeler's identification of the corkwing wrasse at Quanterness, Orkney, where it does not occur now. The sea was probably warmer at that time. Also in Orkney, in the Viking layers of Buckquoy, some bones of the red seabream emerged. This fish is found in the Mediterranean today and thus it can be deduced that the climate was possibly milder during the Viking period. Further, at the same site, Wheeler found that the length estimates of hake, ling and haddock showed the fish were bigger than would be captured in inshore waters today.

He explained this by postulating that modern fishing pressure on the species may have reduced the stock of large fish close to the shore. A different reason was proposed for the retrieval of many large ling from medieval King's Lynn, Norfolk. The present distribution of ling is such that it is very rare in the southern and central North Sea. Dr Wheeler suggests that large ling might have been captured from the region of Flamborough Head, Humberside, and traded with other fishing ports in the North Sea. Conversely, over-exploitation by later generations of man could also account for its scarcity.

Although otoliths are rare finds they were retrieved in some quantity from the middens at Oronsay. By careful sieving it was found that 95 per cent of the total fish bone comprised one species, the saithe or coalfish *(Pollachius virens)*. In an excellent piece of research, published in the *Proceedings of the Prehistoric Society,* 1980, Dr Mellars and Dr Wilkinson demonstrated that otolith length measurements provided evidence that four of the middens had accumulated as a result of seasonal exploitation of the fish. Using data from modern saithe which had been caught at different times of the year, they found a direct correlation between otolith length and fish body length. Previous researchers have demonstrated that, in the first four years of life, growth in the saithe is rapid and the fish can be grouped by body size into age categories with great accuracy. Otoliths and also scales exhibit annual growth rings and Mellars and Wilkinson hope to check their results with further research into this aspect.

7
Preserved bodies

Some of the most spectacular animal finds are the mammoths of Siberia, where permafrost conditions have preserved the carcasses in an excellent condition. Pfizenmayer, in his book *Siberian Man and Mammoths,* describes his journey across Siberian countryside in order to excavate some mammoths which had been discovered by frightened locals. He gives a splendid account of the problems of digging up a large smelly animal together with a useful description of the preserved cadaver. Bodies of Upper Pleistocene horses and woolly rhinoceroses have also been found in the permafrost. A very well preserved carcass of a woolly rhinoceros was found in the salt and petroleum impregnated silt in Starunia on the northern slope of the Carpathian mountains. It is now displayed in the Museum of the Institute of Systematic Zoology, Krakow, Poland.

The Scythian tombs of the Altai mountains, between Siberia and Outer Mongolia, contained the remarkably well preserved corpses of men and horses over two thousand years old. All the horses were geldings between two and twenty years old at death. It is extremely difficult to identify the bones of geldings and this material proved valuable.

A wide range of animals were preserved as mummies by the ancient Egyptians, including crocodiles, fish, beetles, eels, gerbils, bulls, birds and cats. Dr T. G. H. James, in *An Introduction to Ancient Egypt,* points out that animal mummification resulted as a development of the Egyptians' identification of certain gods with animals. In the Ptolemaic and Roman periods there was a great deal of mummification and burial of sacred animals.

Animal cemeteries were situated in the neighbourhood of the appropriate cult centres. Thus Bubastis has large cat cemeteries, being the centre of worship of the cat-goddess Bastet. On the other hand Hermopolis in Middle Egypt has huge ibis cemeteries, the local god being the ibis-headed Thoth. Mummification tended to be poorly performed and quite often only the skeleton was left before the bandages were applied.

Dr P. L. Armitage and Dr J. Clutton-Brock have examined by radiography the mummies of fifty-three cats which were presented to the British Museum by Sir Flinders Petrie in about

1900. Amongst their findings they showed that the cats had mostly died at either four months old or between nine and twelve months old, suggesting that they had been deliberately killed, possibly by strangling, and then had been made into mummies for selling as votive offerings. This contrasts with the picture depicted by the ancient historian Herodotus who said that when a cat died the Egyptian owners shaved their eyebrows in great sorrow (Herodotus II, 67).

Sculpture can give a good idea of what the animals looked like (plate 21), and it is known from wall paintings that some cats were used for fowling in the marshes. There is no doubt that the Egyptians domesticated the cat. From Egypt it was introduced into the British Isles by the Romans.

Plate 21. Egyptian bronze statue of a cat. Roman period, dated after 30 BC. (Copyright: British Museum.)

8
Wool, leather and hair remnants

Dr M. Ryder is the leading authority on research into wool, leather and hair remains. He noted that the arrangement of wool and hair fibres in the skin of sheep was different in the domesticated and wild forms. This prompted an investigation into the history of sheep domestication. Wild sheep have a short, hairy outer coat with a shorter woolly one underneath. The outer hairs are about 60 millimetres (2⅜ inches) in length and are more like bristles; they are called kemps. Since domestication, the fleece has changed so that there is more development of the wool than the kemp. These changes have been brought about by man through selective breeding.

The kemps and woollen fibres can be related to two different follicles in the skin, the primaries and secondaries. The primaries are the first to form, are usually the bigger and are arranged in rows; the secondaries are more numerous and are arranged to one side of the primaries in the domestic sheep. The secondaries are normally the smaller follicles and tend to grow finer fibres than the primaries. Consequently the more secondary follicles a sheep has in its skin, the finer the fleece will be. In wild sheep, the secondary follicles quite often lie between the primaries.

Skin and hair are well preserved in acid waterlogged conditions such as peat bogs and also in arid climates in the Near East. Dr Ryder has further investigated the remains of parchment, which in Britain is mainly made out of sheepskin.

In Britain there has been no survival of wool or sheepskin from the neolithic period. The earliest wool belongs to the bronze age and closely approximates to the fibre diameters of the feral Soay sheep; it was naturally pigmented. Ryder made two observations about iron age European wool. First, he found a fibre in addition to the two main types already discussed, a long continuously growing or heterotype fibre. Heterotypes are intermediate between kemp and wool; they are coarse and kemp-like in summer but thin and wool-like in winter. Secondly, the other great change in European iron age wool was that it lacked a natural pigment.

Ryder has found that some Danish wools from the northern border of the Roman Empire are finer than actual Roman examples. On Romano-British sites the range of fleece types is represented by sheep of a Soay type, i.e. a hairy medium wool and a generalised medium wool, as well as by finer fleeces of medium wool and true fine wool.

The application of similar studies to leather is beset with difficulty since the wild ancestor, the aurochs *(Bos primigenius)*, is extinct. Also the coats of modern domestic cattle vary less than the fleeces of sheep, presumably because there has been little or no selective breeding for different coat types.

Hair remains from Roman and medieval leather demonstrate a coat similar to modern cattle with micron hair dimensions. However a neolithic bow from Meare, Somerset, dated to 2600 BC, had bovine hairs much finer than those of modern cattle. Quite often bronze age people buried their dead in cow hides. While some hides had hair diameters similar to modern types, a few Scottish examples exhibited finer hairs.

9
Coprolites and parasites

Coprolites are desiccated or fossilised dung and occur mainly on New World archaeological sites where arid conditions prevail. The humid climate of the British Isles does not favour their preservation. An analysis of their contents can reveal information concerning dietary practices, health, seasonal, environmental and climatic factors.

It is not always easy to distinguish between animal and human faecal remains, although Callen has pioneered a helpful method. Specimens are immersed in a dilute solution of trisodium phosphate for a minimum of seventy-two hours. If the coprolite is of human origin, the fluid becomes opaque, dark brown or black, while if it originates from a carnivorous or herbivorous mammal the fluid remains translucent. This approach does not always give satisfactory results so Callen suggested the following guides: coprolite shape, size, smell and contents.

After immersion in the sodium triphosphate solution the material is then sieved while being washed with distilled water. The sample is examined microscopically and further residue extracted from the liquid fraction via centrifugation.

Callen's description of the Tehuacan coprolites in Byers's book *The Prehistory of the Tehuacan Valley* results from a meticulous analysis. Hair from the human faeces was identified to faunal species and revealed that the humans had eaten cottontail rabbits, pocket gophers, white-tailed deer and ring-tailed cats. The hair hints that the animals had been eaten with their skins on.

Coprolites are also a good source for insect and parasite remains. Parasites are useful in archaeological contexts as they can give information about the antiquity of pests and diseases, both human and animal. This can be related to the environmental conditions. Human coprolite, dated 100 BC to AD 500, from north-western Germany contained common intestinal round-worms, whipworms, tapeworms and liver flukes.

10
Animal miscellany

Amphibian and reptile bones are rarely recovered from excavations. The European pond tortoise *(Emys orbicularis)* occurred in Britain and Europe during previous interglacials, to the north and west of its present breeding range. This is indicative of warmer climatic conditions than are being experienced today.

Amphibians were occasionally consumed by the Romans, for example frogs' legs. Evidence of this practice emerged from the sites of Augst and Ersingen-Murain in Switzerland and Pforzheim in Germany.

A great many ritual pits have been excavated on Gallic and Gallo-Roman sites, particularly in Aquitaine, dating from 50 to 30 BC. They are characterised not only by cremations and funerary offerings including pottery and domestic animal bones, but also by creatures in the form of insectivores and amphibians. The practice continued into the fourth century AD. A good example is the fourth-century Montmaurin villa, where four pits revealed three insectivores, including the greater white-toothed shrew, sixteen rodents represented by water, field and red-backed voles, and seventy-two amphibians (toads and frogs).

An unusual animal to turn up in a Roman sewer at York was the remains of a sponge. Spicules of one or more species of marine sponge occurred abundantly. The Romans used sponge fragments on sticks as toilet paper (Martial, *Epigrams* 12, 48, 7).

Acarology or the study of mites is a field that is being developed. Mites are useful for describing immediate environmental conditions and are widely distributed, but identification difficulties have led to a lack of use.

Finally, it is apposite to note that the Romans' curiosity could be aroused by ancient animal remains. Professor E. Schmid discovered a mammoth tooth in the Roman levels at Augusta Raurica, Augst, Switzerland.

11
Glossary

Aeolian deposits: those laid down by the wind.

Amino-acids: these are the fundamental constituents of living matter; they are the building blocks for proteins.

Anaerobic: an environment where oxygen is lacking.

Artefact: any archaeological find thought to have been formed by man, e.g. bones, pots or flints.

Beam: main axis of an antler.

bc: uncalibrated radiocarbon dates.

BC: calibrated radiocarbon dates stated in calendar years.

bp: before present.

Bronze age: the prehistoric period following the neolithic, and during which bronze was used for tools and weapons.

Cementum: a bone-like substance deposited at the teeth roots of vertebrates. The rate of deposition varies over the year and gives a banded appearance.

Chitin: a nitrogenous polysaccharide of immense strength and chemical resistance, found in the cuticle of insects.

Collagen: a major constituent of bone and a fibrous protein which on boiling yields gelatin.

Coprolite: fossilised faeces.

Dendrochronology: dating by examination and counting of annual growth rings in tree remains. The relative widths of rings give additional information on climatic changes.

Dimorphism: existing in two forms; e.g. male and female animals.

Distal: the part of a bone situated far from the place of attachment; the opposite to proximal.

Domestication: the management of animals so that they can be bred primarily for the advantage of man.

Epiphysis: the separately ossified end of a growing bone which is attached to the shaft by cartilage. When bone growth is completed, the epiphysis fuses to the shaft.

Exoskeleton: a skeleton covering the outside of the body or situated in the skin; e.g. the cuticle of insects.

Fauna: the animals of a region or epoch.

Feral: domestic animal now living in the wild.

Fluviatile deposit: one laid down by a river.

Foramen: a hole in a bone completely surrounded by that bone. (Plural: foramina.)

Fossil: the remains of an organism whose hard parts only are preserved, usually partly or wholly replaced by minerals deposited from circulating water.

Frontal: a pair of skull bones covering the front part of the brain in vertebrates.

Frontlet: a term coined by Professor J. G. D. Clark for describing the Star Carr red deer antler masks.

Iconography: the study of pictures, statuary and portraits.

Indigenous: native to a particular area, not introduced.

Insectivores: primitive insect-eating group, e.g. mole, hedgehog and shrew.

Iron age: the prehistoric period characterised by the widespread use of iron for tools and weapons.

Isotope: isotopes are atoms with different atomic masses but the same atomic number (i.e. number of protons or electrons) and identical chemical properties: e.g. chlorine has two stable isotopes, chlorine-35 and chlorine-37. (See *Mass spectrometer.*)

Lacustrine deposit: one laid down by a lake.

Leaching: the removal of soluble salts by rainwater flushing through the soil.

Levalloisian: the Levallois technique is a method of flint working employed by certain Lower Palaeolithic and more generally Middle Palaeolithic hand-axe makers.

Lower Palaeolithic: the part of the old stone age before the evolution of modern man, *Homo sapiens sapiens.*

Mass spectrometer: an instrument that measures the ratio of mass to electrical charge for atomic particles. It works by stripping electrons off neutral atoms, so producing ions, which are then fired through a magnetic field where they follow a circular path whose radius is proportional to mass divided by charge. Since ions of different fully ionised isotopes of the same element have the same charge but different masses they are separable.

Mean (statistical): average. Strictly, the mean of a set of measurements of the same type of quantity (e.g. lengths of bone, heights of people) is the sum of the measurements divided by the number of measurements summed.

Mesolithic: the prehistoric period immediately following the ice age, and during which people existed by hunting and gathering.

Midden: a refuse heap or mound.

Mummy: the body of a human or an animal embalmed according to the rites practised in ancient Egypt.

Neolithic: the period of prehistoric farming before the introduction of metalworking.

Palaeolithic: the stone age period when people lived by hunting and food gathering and had no knowledge of farming or the use of metals.

Parabolic curve: roughly, a curve of shape similar to a section through the centre of a torch reflector, or the shape of a glacial valley. Strictly, a curve whose equation may be typified by an equation of the form $y = ax^2 + bx + c$.

Parietal: a pair of skull bones which cover a large part of the upper surface of the brain, behind the frontal bone.

Permafrost: permanently frozen ground.

Pleistocene: a geological epoch, known more popularly as the Great Ice Age. In archaeological terms all the palaeolithic cultures fall within this period.

Polarised light: light may be regarded as a wave phenomenon. 'Ordinary' light is unpolarised, the direction in which the waves vibrate being completely random. Polarising filters (as in polaroid sunglasses) preferentially transmit wave vibrations in one direction and completely block perpendicular waves, producing polarised light. Some 'light' sources, such as television transmitters, produce polarised waves directly.

Polled: hornless.

Population (statistical): the entire collection of objects about which one is attempting to make general deductions, from measurements of a sample of those objects.

Potassium-argon dating: the isotope potassium-40 decays to argon-40 at a known rate. Measurement of the ratio of potassium-40 to argon-40 can reveal the age of a specimen if the original relative concentration is known or can be separately deduced.

Proto-Maglemosian: the Maglemosian was the first mesolithic culture of the North European Plain. 'Proto' means an early developmental stage of the Maglemosian.

Ptolemaic: the period in Egyptian history from 332 to 30 BC. After 30 BC, Egypt became a Roman province.

Ritual pit: 'ritual' or 'votive' are terms used in archaeology for artefacts whose form, grouping or position cannot be explained on grounds of usefulness to the owners or creators.

Significance (statistical): a measure of the unlikeliness of a statistical result having come about purely by chance. For example, if the age of one hundred people chosen at random from a building was found to be eight years old, this is very unlikely to be so purely by chance. The building is probably a primary school!

Species: the smallest unit of classification commonly used. The group whose members have the greatest mutual resemblance.

Spicule: small hard body, especially in the framework of a sponge.

Steer: castrated bullock.

Stratigraphy: this is an important concept, adopted from geology. Where a deposit overlies another, the upper must have accumulated later in time than the lower.

Taphonomy: a study of the factors affecting the degree of completeness of recovery of an animal's remains, from the time of the demise of the animal to its being excavated.

Upper Palaeolithic: the part of the old stone age in which modern man emerged as *Homo sapiens sapiens*.

Votive offering: see *Ritual pit.*

Variance (statistical): a measure of the spread of the value of a property. In general there are two components of measured variance, one due to random measurement errors and one due to inherent differences in the items being measured. For example, an old brick factory might produce nominal 9 inch bricks which are actually between 8½ and 9½ inches long. If measured carelessly with a slightly stretchy tape measure even a set of exactly 9 inch bricks would produce a range of measured lengths. Both factors would contribute to the measured variance.

Velvet: furry skin covering the antlers as they grow.

Weathering: disintegration of rocks or bone by exposure to the atmosphere.

X-ray crystallography: the study of the arrangement of atoms in crystalline solids by observing the scattering of beams of X-rays directed through the material.

Zooarchaeologist: a person who studies animal remains from archaeological sites with the aim of understanding man's past.

12
Further reading

Armitage, P. L. and Clutton-Brock, J. 'A System for Classification and Description of the Horn Cores of Cattle from Archaeological Sites'. *Journal of Archaeological Science* 3 (1976), 329-48.

Armitage, P. L. and Clutton-Brock, J. 'A Radiological and Histological Investigation into the Mummification of Cats from Ancient Egypt'. *Journal of Archaeological Science* 8 (1981).

Brothwell, D. and Higgs, E. S. *Science in Archaeology*. London, 1969.

Brown, G. T. *Dentition as Indicative of the Age of the Animals of the Farm*. London, 1927.

Byers, D. S. *The Prehistory of the Tehuacan Valley. Volume 1: Environment and Subsistence*. University of Texas Press, 1967.

Chaplin, R. E. *The Study of Animal Bones from Archaeological Sites*. London, 1971.

Clark, J. G. D. *Star Carr: A Case Study in Bioarchaeology*. Addison-Wesley Modula Publications, number 10, 1972.

Cornwall, I. W. *Bones for the Archaeologist*. London, 1956.

Driesch, A. v. d. 'A Guide to the Measurement of Animal Bones from Archaeological Sites'. *Peabody Museum Bulletin* 1. Harvard University, 1976.

Evans, J. G. *Land Snails in Archaeology with Special Reference to the British Isles*. London, 1972.

Evans, J. G. *The Environment of Early Man in the British Isles*. Elek Books Ltd, 1975.

Grant, A. 'Use of Tooth Wear as a Guide to the Age of Domestic Animals' in *Excavations at Portchester Castle*, Volume 1, edited by B. W. Cunliffe, 1975.

Grayson, K. 'Minimum Numbers and Sample Size in Vertebrate Faunal Analysis'. *American Antiquity* 43 (1978), 53-65.

Handbooks for the Identification of British Insects. Royal Entomological Society, 1950.

Higham, C. F. W. 'The Metrical Attributes of Two Samples of Bovine Limb Bones'. *Journal of Zoology* 157 (1969), 63-74.

Higham, C. F. W. and Message, M. 'An Assessment of a Prehistoric Technique of Bovine Husbandry' in *Science in Archaeology*, edited by Brothwell and Higgs (1969).

Howard, M. M. 'The Metrical Determination of the Metapodials and Skulls of Cattle' in *Man and Cattle*, edited by Mourant and Zeuner. London, 1963.

Jewell, P. A. 'Cattle from British Archaeological Sites' in *Man and Cattle*, edited by Mourant and Zeuner. London, 1963.

Joy, N. H. *A Practical Handbook of British Beetles*. London, 1932.

Kerney, M. P. and Cameron, R. A. D. *A Field Guide to the Land Snails of Britain and North-west Europe*. 1979.

King, K. 'Gamma-Carboxyglutamic Acid in Fossil Bones and Its Significance for Amino-Acid Dating'. *Nature* 273 (1978), 41-3.

Luff, R-M. *A Zooarchaeological Study of the Roman North-western Provinces*. British Archaeological Reports, International Series 137, 1982.

Mellars, P. A. *The Early Postglacial Settlement of Northern Europe*. Duckworth, 1978.

Mellars, P. A. and Wilkinson, M. 'Fish Otoliths as Evidence of Seasonality in Prehistoric Shell Middens: The Evidence from Oronsay'. *Proceedings of the Prehistoric Society* 46 (1980), 9-44.

Noddle, B. A. 'Some Minor Skeletal Differences in Sheep', in *Research Problems in Zooarchaeology* edited by Brothwell, Thomas and Clutton-Brock. *Institute of Archaeology Occasional Publication* number 3 (1978), 133-9.

Oakley, K. P. 'Relative Dating of the Fossil Hominids of Europe'. *Bulletin of the British Museum, Natural History Geology* volume 34 part 1.

Osborne, P. J. 'An Insect Fauna from the Roman Site of Alcester, Warwickshire'. *Britannia* 2 (1971), 156-65.

Ovey, C. D. (editor). 'The Swanscombe Skull. A Survey of Research on a Pleistocene Site'. *Royal Anthropological Institute Occasional Paper* number 20 (1964).

Payne, S. 'On the Interpretation of Bone Samples from Archaeological Sites', in *Papers in Economic Prehistory,* edited by E. S. Higgs, London, 1972.

Payne, S. 'Kill-off Patterns in Sheep and Goats: The Mandibles from Asvan Kale'. *Journal of Anatolian Studies* 23 (1973), 281-303.

Pfizenmayer, E. W. *Siberian Man and Mammoths.* London, 1939. (Translated from the German by M. D. Simpson.)

Ryder, M. L. *Animal Bones in Archaeology.* Oxford and Edinburgh, 1968.

Ryder, M. L. 'Livestock', in *The Agrarian History of England and Wales,* edited by S. Piggott. Cambridge University Press, 1981.

Schmid, E. *Atlas of Animal Bones/Knochenatlas.* Elsevier, 1972.

Shackleton, N. J. 'Marine Molluscs in Archaeology', in *Science in Archaeology* edited by Brothwell and Higgs. London, 1969, 407-14.

Silver, I. A. 'The Ageing of Domestic Animals', in *Science in Archaeology* edited by Brothwell and Higgs. London, 1969.

Sutcliffe, A. J. and Zeuner, F. E. 'Excavations in the Torbryan Caves, Devonshire: 1, Torenewton Cave'. *Proceedings of the Devon Archaeological and Exploration Society* 5 (1958), 127-45.

Watson, J. P. N. 'The Interpretation of Epiphysial Fusion Data', in *Research Problems in Zooarchaeology* edited by Brothwell, Thomas and Clutton-Brock. *Institute of Archaeology Occasional Publication* number 3 (1978), 97-101.

Wheeler, A. 'Problems of Identification and Interpretation of Archaeological Fish Remains', in *Research Problems in Zooarchaeology* edited by Brothwell, Thomas and Clutton-Brock. *Institute of Archaeology Occasional Publication* number 3 (1978), 69-75.

Index

The page numbers in italic type refer to illustrations.